GREY OWL

THE INCREDIBLE STORY
OF ARCHIE BELANEY
1888-1938

GEOFF HUTCHINSON

Illustrations by Dave Brown

© Geoff Hutchinson 1985

Acknowledgements

Much has been written about Grey Owl. Many fine books and articles have been published on the life of the Hastings lad who went to Canada and eventually became a national figure, famed for his books on wildlife, his lectures and his fight to preserve the beaver from extinction.

It is not my intention to try and better these publications, or to enter into any deep analytical survey of the subject. As a Hastings person I felt I would like to put the story, as accurately as I could, into a compressed form so, hopefully, passing on the fascinating story to more people who do not wish to be weighed down with the 'heavier' versions.

However, if after reading this booklet, one is fired to find out more detail, further information may be obtained from the excellent book by Lovat Dickson, Grey Owl's publisher and biographer, entitled *Wilderness Man: The Strange Story of Grey Owl,* the book by his Indian 'wife' Anahareo *Grey Owl and I* and, of course, the books written by Grey Owl himself.

My special thanks go to Mr Lovat Dickson, for permission to use material from *Wilderness Man,* Mr Stan Winters for the foreword, The Ontario Heritage Foundation, The Canadian High Commission, Macmillan Publishers Ltd, The Ottawa Public Library, Karsh Photographic Studios, the Hastings Reference Library and the Sussex Records Office, Lewes for their valuable assistance, Mr Ian Dobson for sowing the seed, Mr Dave Brown for the illustrations and design, Mr Tony Daley for his patience, and Jan Roadnight for her help and encouragement.

Geoff Hutchinson
1985

Other titles by same author:
FULLER
The life and times of John Fuller of Brightling, 1757-1834
THE MARY STANFORD DISASTER
The story of a lifeboat, November 15th, 1928
BAIRD
The story of John Logie Baird, 1888-1946
THE LOVERS' SEAT
The history and the love story of 1786. Fact and fiction

Body copy set in 9/10pt Palatino Roman by the author

Contents

Foreword by Mr Stan Winters	page 4
Introduction	5
The Belaney family	7
Boyhood in Hastings	10
Canada: The first steps	13
Hell-raising in Bisco	15
The army and an English wife	17
Renewing old acquaintances	18
Anahareo	20
McGinnis and McGinty	23
Fame and the saving of the beaver	25
Lectures in Britain and America	29
Summary	32

FOREWORD

This is, truly, a great honor to be asked by Mr Hutchinson to write the foreword for his booklet on Grey Owl.

Mr Hutchinson is to be commended for his condensation of the history of Grey Owl (Archie Belaney) and his very outstanding career. I was very privileged to have known Grey Owl, and lived with him at Beaver Lodge on Ajawaan in the Prince Albert National Park. My first meeting with Grey Owl took place in August and September 1932 when Anahareo and her new born daughter, Shirley Dawn, came to the Winters' home in Prince Albert and Archie came in from Ajawaan to see the newest of the Belaney family.

In 1936, when Grey Owl was writing *Tales of an Empty Cabin*, I spent the summer with him. My sister, Margaret, typed his book and I looked after the beaver, did the cooking and tended to the tourists. We thought, at the time, it was quite a hardship for two teenagers to be in the wilderness, but on looking back now it was actually one of the highlights of our lives.

Grey Owl was a conservationist, a naturalist, a writer, story teller and a very good friend. It was a sad day for the Winters family when Grey Owl died in 1938. We attended his funeral service in Prince Albert.

Congratulations, Mr Hutchinson, on a fine résumé of Wa-Sha-Quon-Asin (He-who-walks-by-night). I salute you.

Stan Winters

Stan Winters
Prince Albert
Saskatchewan
Canada
1985

INTRODUCTION

Eccentricity is surely one of the most fascinating aspects of the human condition. The English seem to have a knack of throwing up the character with the driving inner spirit which forces him to break with all convention. A person who seems to be out of time and enters into a lifestyle different from the one expected of him. It makes for fascinating study!

The story of Archibald Stansfeld Belaney is such a story, and as it unfolds one cannot help to be amazed at the number of miles a person will travel in search of dreams, and just how much can be crammed into a brief lifespan of 50 years.

The story begins at the turn of the century in Victorian England and ends during the 1930s amid the beautiful vast open spaces and forests of Saskatchewan in Canada.

It tells of an English boy from a broken home, who was raised by his two spinster aunts in Hastings and who was eventually to become a national hero in Canada during the 1930s, and to become known and acclaimed as a full-blooded Indian with the name of Grey Owl (Wa-Sha-Quon-Asin — He-who-walks-by-night), writer, lecturer, conservationist and the saviour of the threatened beaver.

It is a truly fascinating tale and as a starting point we will look at his ancestry, where one can almost certainly spot the family traits which undoubtedly had a great bearing on his subsequent behaviour.

The story of Archibald Stansfeld Belaney . . .

Remember you belong to Nature, not it to you
Grey Owl

THE BELANEY FAMILY

The origins of the Belaney family are in Berwickshire, in the Lowlands of Scotland. At the beginning of the 19th century John Belaney was a successful farmer with a large family of 10 children. At least two of his sons attended university and three of them had a flirtation with literature, as they pursued their various careers, and had their works published. James Belaney produced a lengthy poem entitled *The Steeplechase* in 1837 and in 1841 *A Treatise on Falconry* was published. The Rev Robert Belaney wrote books on ecclesiastical matters and Archibald Belaney produced a book of verse entitled *The 100 Days of Napoleon.*

Archibald Belaney, the grandfather of the subject of this booklet, went into business in the City of London and became a prosperous ship's broker. He married a young heiress named Juliana Jackson and they had three children, George, Caroline and Adelaide. The family moved from the centre of London to Croydon, which in those days had a country air about it, and settled into a well-appointed house.

Archibald died in the first year of residence, but the family were left well provided for and stayed there for another 19 years.

On leaving school, George, a totally spoilt son, was found a job in a tea and coffee importing business. He was to stay in London during the week and return home at weekends. However, after two years, George expressed to his mother that he was dissatisfied with the job and very much wanted to be his own master and run his own importing business. His sister Adelaide, who disliked him intensely, suggested to her mother that George was merely using this as an excuse to do less work and have more time off. Her mother wouldn't listen and with her financial help George was set up in his own business in 1879.

George had all the grandiose ideas but not the resolve to carry them through. During time he should have spent running the business he journeyed to South Africa with a friend on a big game hunt. He was gone for six months. This frivolous attitude to his business affairs proved disastrous and within a year the company had gone into liquidation, yet still his mother, ever-eager to see him succeed, was seeking other avenues for him to explore.

After the failure of his business he went to Suffolk to stay with his hunting companion. George told his mother there were employment opportunities there and this she believed. However, during this visit, punctuated with much drinking and debauchery, he became involved with Rose Hines, the daughter of a tavern keeper. She became pregnant, and at the insistence of the girl's mother, George was obliged to marry her, the marriage taking place on April 13, 1881 at Diss, Norfolk. On December 9 of that same year a daughter was born, named Rose Ethel Belaney. The child survived 18 months and by that time George had disappeared, and divorce from Rose Hines must have eventually followed. His mother had no knowledge whatsoever of this episode in his life.

Before this escapade in Norfolk, George had fallen in love with Elizabeth Cox. He wanted to marry her but his mother had told him he must first carve a career out for himself before contemplating such an idea.

After leaving Rose Hines, he left England for America, taking Elizabeth with him. Once in America he indulged himself in more game-shooting, and in Florida turned his hand to taxidermy.

During the time there Elizabeth gave birth to a daughter, Gertrude.

George and family had to return to England when Elizabeth fell ill and during this time he asked his mother to buy some land in Florida where he could grow oranges. She agreed but insisted this was his last chance to succeed at her expense. She was at last beginning to get the picture. He had become a total disappointment to her.

So on November 18, 1885, accompanied by the now recovered Elizabeth and her 12-year-old sister Katherine, he set sail for America again.

Within one year Elizabeth had died and in the following year, 1886, he married her sister Katherine, then aged 13. In June 1888 he suddenly sold his land, left his three-year-old daughter with neighbours, and returned to England with his then pregnant wife.

Since George had been in America the Belaney family had moved to 52 St Helens Wood Road, in Hastings. He had written to his mother explaining what he had done and requesting her to put them up. His mother was none too happy about this situation, but nevertheless she agreed they could come to Hastings and she would rent a house for them for a few months, during which time George must find a job. However, George did not try over-hard to find employment. He hated England, and he especially hated Hastings. He was restless, all the time wanting to travel. A dreamer, a waster and a parasite.

On September 18, 1888, in Hastings, Archibald Stansfeld Belaney was born.

Young Archie

Boyhood in Hastings

Two years later a second son, Hugh, was born. George was still in a very unhappy state. He was still sponging off his mother and seemed incapable of holding down a job for any sensible period of time. All he wanted to do was get away from the confines of the family ties. He felt trapped.

At this stage it would appear his mother at last lost her patience. A document was drawn up by the family's solicitor, which George was persuaded to sign. It stated that George should go into exile. He would be allowed a small income provided he never came back to England again. His wife was also required to sign the document and she had to declare never to see him again. She would be allowed a comfortable income to bring up her two sons and it was deemed that this would be the best solution for all concerned, and so George and Katherine parted.

Archie was four years old at the time and old enough to appreciate the fact that his father was leaving and might never return. It was a tremendous wrench for him and a time of much sadness.

George left for America and Katherine never saw him again, although he wrote to her on a couple of occasions soon after the parting, asking her for money. This she supplied, a fact that was discovered by the Belaney family causing them to cut off her allowance, and take young Archie into their care to ensure he could lead a good life. Katherine would only be allowed to see him at their discretion.

And so Archie was taken into the care of his grandmother and her two middle-aged spinster daughters, Ada and Carrie, into the starchy atmosphere of their Victorian home.

Archie was to see his mother only twice during his boyhood, once when he was dangerously ill with pneumonia and once when he spent a holiday with her and his younger brother Hugh at Worthing.

The Belaney family explained the situation thus: that Kitty could not manage both boys, Hugh would go to London with his mother, and Grandmother Belaney would undertake the task of raising Archie and pay for his education.

Twelve years after Katherine and George parted, she heard that he had died in Mexico, and she became married to a Mr Scott-Brown. All in all it seems that Katherine had received a very rough deal from the Belaney family.

In 1895 Grandmother Belaney and her two daughters moved from St Helen's Wood Road to 36 St Mary's Terrace, in Hastings.

It would appear that during his childhood a love-hate relationship developed between Archie and his Aunt Ada, the more dominating of the two sisters. She was to be both his mother and father. He worshipped his grandmother and she returned all the love in a very firm but fair way. As a child he was fascinated by nature and was allowed to keep a menagerie in his attic room. Rabbits, snakes, toads and weasels lived in the room at various times.

His other great enthusiasm was music and his aunts taught him how to play the piano. His love of classical music was never to leave him. With his music and love of animals he seemed to escape from the world around him and as he grew older a loner instinct developed in him.

In September 1899 the time had come for him to join the Hastings Grammar School, then in nearby Nelson Road. At school he was regarded very much as an odd character. He was described as an eccentric in the school's magazine. He was fascinated by woods and wild animals, and would often walk to school with a snake or fieldmouse in his pocket. He would imitate the hooting of an owl, and many thought him to be more like a Red Indian than a respectable Grammar School boy.

He loved reading about Indians and the Wild West. This was the time when children's magazines were full of Wild West stories, and children delighted in acting out scenes of battles between Cowboys and Indians. But to young Archie it was not a game. It was a serious business. His hobby was silent tracking — to move unobserved — and he developed a skill at tracking animals, crawling along on his tummy, and imagining himself to be an Indian in the forest, as he spent many hours in the St Helen's Woods, a large area of woodland situated north of his home. He also spent much time in the beautiful Fairlight Glen on the outskirts of Hastings. He would tell his schoolmates he had Indian blood in his veins.

The other boys at school thought him very strange. They would laugh about him behind his back — but never to his face. There was something in him they did not understand, or trust.

It must have been difficult for him living with his two aunts and grandmother instead of his own parents. How did he explain to his schoolmates why he lived as he did? Possibly the story of his Indian ancestry was a protective shield against prying questions. As his school days approached an end he expressed an ambition to go to Canada and join the Indians, study them and write about them, and he put this idea to his aunts. They, of course, were horrified to think of him throwing away his education and embarking on such a madcap venture as this, but after months of persistence by Archie they realised he had a genuine dream to carry out these plans. A compromise was struck. He would stay at home until he was 17, work in Hastings for one year and then, if he still wished to go, the family would agree, on the proviso that he would go to Canada as a farming student.

So, on leaving school, Archie took a job as a clerk with a firm of timber merchants, Cheale Brothers of London Road, St Leonards. His tasks included checking timber going in and out of the company. The monotony of the job was to drive him to distraction. He hated it. He longed for the outdoor life, and eventually devised a devilish plan to rid himself of the job. Unfortunately for the company it was to mean a temporary end for them as well. He climbed onto the roof and lowered gunpowder down the chimney, an extremely dangerous thing to do. The resulting explosion practically demolished the building and with it the job he detested so much.

During all of that year he was training himself for the existence he dreamed of. He would go without food or water for two days at a time, he slept on the hard floor of his bedroom, and some nights would go into the garden where he would sleep in a tree with just a blanket for cover.

The year was 1905 and he was now 17. He was tall, slender and handsome and possessed a sharp sense of humour. His aunts thought if he were to meet a young lady it would extinguish the desire to go to Canada and he would settle down and create a life for himself and his partner in England.

Through his aunts' manoeuvring, he was introduced to a girl named Connie Holmes, very pretty and two years his junior. He was attracted to her and they had a brief flirtation, but women were not part of Archie's plans at this particular moment and his mind thought only of his adventure to the new life in Canada.

When the year of the compromise was up the Belaney sisters still resisted. They did not want Archie to go at the beginning of the severe Canadian winter, and it was finally agreed he could leave the following spring.

At last, on a March afternoon in 1906, Archie left the Liverpool docks aboard the steamship *Canada*. He waved farewell to his Aunt Ada who had gone to see him off, his mind totally engaged with the challenge ahead.

The adventure had begun.

CANADA:
THE FIRST STEPS

Archie Belaney sailed into Canada on April 6, 1906, and landed at Halifax, giving his destination as Toronto.

Little is known about his early days in Canada, but it is believed that he travelled to Toronto and took work as a clerk in a large Toronto department store. He did not enjoy the work but it gave him a much-needed salary. He stayed there for four months and then headed northwards intending to travel to Cobalt, where silver had been discovered three years earlier. However, it is believed that on a sudden impulse, he left the train at Temiskaming, 30 miles south of Cobalt, on the Quebec/Ontario borders.

Here he met a well-known colourful character named Bill Guppy and asked him for work. Guppy was a guide who took tourists into the woods on hunting and fishing trips and he was in the process of building his own camp on Lake Temagami.

Archie told him he was broke and would love to learn guiding, or indeed, anything that would take him into the woods.

The two men made a deal. Archie would work for his food during the coming winter and in the spring Guppy would take him into the woods and teach him the art of guiding. Archie lived with the Guppy family during that winter and was very popular with them. Bill taught him how to trap, and was impressed with Archie's way with wild animals. He noticed that Archie was a born hunter, but did not seem to enjoy the actual killing — a feeling which would never leave him.

Archie got to know the country and learned a great deal from an old Indian who was in the employ of Guppy. On one occasion the two of them visited Bear Island Camp, the headquarters of the Ojibway Indians. Archie was fascinated by these people and listened intently to their conversations, trying to piece together odd phrases that they were saying.

During the summer of 1907 Archie worked as a canoeman and guide for Bill Guppy, and in the autumn Guppy found him a job as a mail carrier between Temiskaming and Temagami. During the summer Archie had spent his time with rich tourists and was now eager to mix with the Indian friends he had made, and to learn more of their ways and master their language. He had become particularly friendly with a man named Tommy Saville, an Englishman, who had come to Canada in much the same circumstances as himself, and who was living as an Indian and had an Indian wife. Archie was introduced to the elders of the tribe, men such as Old Pete Misabi and Ned White Bear, who taught him their Indian skills and related stories of their past. He learned much from them.

When Bill Guppy saw Archie again in 1908 he noticed how he had changed, and adopted the Indian ways. His appearance bore the mark of the Indian. His hair was tied at the back of his head by a strip of hide, his face was weathered, and he wore moccasins instead of boots. He even changed his walk and his command of the Ojibway language was improving all the time.

It was while he was employed as a mail carrier he first met Angele Eguena, an Indian girl. He found her company pleasurable and in 1908 he applied for a licence to marry her. The licence was issued but the wedding did not take place. Archie, for some reason, suddenly disappeared. Something he had done had offended the Indians and turned them against him. It has been suggested that he probably tried to sample the pleasures of marriage before the actual wedding and if so this would certainly have been frowned upon.

It was in this year of 1908 that he returned briefly to England to visit his family at Hastings. His grandmother had been very ill and he was anxious to see her. However, he found the restricting atmosphere of Hastings too much to bear and although he was not happy about leaving while his grandmother was so ill, he longed to return to his Indian friends in the country he had come to love so well; and after three months he returned to Canada.

He arrived back in Temagami and made up his differences with the Indians. His marriage to Angele was on again and with Tommy Saville as best man, the wedding took place on August 23, 1910 at the Forest Rangers Hall.

From this point on he was totally committed to the Indian way of life. He gave up guiding and cut himself off from the white man's world. He developed a fierce pride which caused him to become argumentative and morose when in the company of white men, defending the Indian with a single-minded passion bordering on the irrational. He began to gain a reputation of being a hard man. He seemed pleased to think his behaviour was disturbing to visitors. He loved to shock people with his profanity. He behaved like a man with an enormous chip on his shoulder.

Archie and Angele started their married life living in a tent on Bear Island and in April a little girl was born. She was named Agnes Belaney.

In the autumn of 1911, finding himself desperately short of money, he went to work in a mine on White Bear Lake. He stuck at this job for only six weeks and left, with a band of Indians, for Lake Abitibi, 150 miles due north, leaving his wife and baby behind.

He returned to Temagami in the spring of 1912. He was in a very unhappy state of mind. He was still short of money, totally dejected and regularly sank into moods of deep depression.

The reason for this must have been the news he had received from England on May 7, 1912, telling him of his grandmother's death. Archie had loved her very much and a feeling of great loss overcame him.

He told his wife he was going to Biscotasing, 120 miles to the west to work as a fire-ranger in the Mississauga Forest Reserve. He told her he would be back in the autumn and promised to send her money in the meantime.

However, he did not keep this promise and it was to be six years before she would see her husband again.

Hell-raising in Bisco

In June, 1912, Archie started his job with the fire-ranging service and set out for the Mississagua Forest Reserve to take up his post for the summer. He enjoyed the work and got on well with his colleagues. They took him to be a white man with a dash of Indian blood in his veins, and he was a very popular member of the fire-ranging team. He was a natural showman. He enjoyed showing off the skills he had learned from the Indians. He revelled in the art of knife-throwing and he loved being the centre of attention, and when the autumn came and he was paid off, he could not face the thought of returning to his wife and child at Temagami.

He decided to spend the winter trapping. Biscotasing was one of the main centres of the fur trade in Northern Ontario. While he was getting his supplies together he took lodgings at a hotel run by a Mrs Legace and he was very comfortable and happy there. It was a bawdy, lively type of establishment used mainly by trappers in the same circumstances as Archie. Happy evenings were spent as he played piano and swapped stories.

However, he could not keep his mind off the Indians, and as he viewed their living conditions compared to his, it made him angry. He saw them as being oppressed and tried to stir them into protest. He became even more antagonistic towards the white man and as a personal protest began to speak Ojibway constantly, pretending not to understand English. He spoke much of his father's exploits in Mexico and his Apache mother. The people of Biscotasing must have been easily fooled! One could not possibly have learned how to play the piano in an Indian camp, or quote Shakespeare and other famous authors and poets with such panache.

For two winters Archie worked as a trapper out of Biscotasing and in the summer was employed by the Forestry Department. He liked the town of Biscotasing. The place was so right for him. He began to build a reputation of being a hell-raiser, a hard drinker and a man who loved to impress an audience with his skill with knives and sharp-shooting. He spent much of his time in the company of young people. They looked upon him as a kind of god, and hung on every word he uttered. He enjoyed his time in Biscotasing, and all the time he pushed thoughts of returning to his family to the back of his mind.

During the second winter season's trapping he took with him as a partner, a young Indian girl named Marie Girard. When they returned to Biscotasing in the spring of 1914, she was pregnant, and Archie stayed in town for only a week before abandoning her and setting off for another job with the Ontario

Forestry Department.

He was employed as assistant to a man named Bill Draper. Their job took them into very remote country during the summer of 1914. Draper was 10 years older than Archie, and was just as wild a character. He could outdrink Archie, tell even taller stories, was a master with a canoe and the two of them formed a close friendship. Their task was to clear out prospectors from the towns along the banks of the Goulais River, and they would very often go for weeks without seeing anyone.

While working their way down the river on September 12, they chanced to meet two timber cutters who told them war had been declared between the British Empire and Germany. On hearing this, Draper, an ex-Royal Navy man, could hardly wait to get into the action and they quickly returned to Biscotasing, arriving there at the end of September 1914.

In the town of Biscotasing Archie could sense that an air of antagonism had built up against him during his absence. People despised the way he had treated Marie Girard. Their attitude seemed to make Archie worse and more arrogant. He got into many arguments and during one, he behaved threateningly with a knife and the law was sent for.

Archie, warned of this, had time for one final act of defiance. He unslung his rifle from his shoulder, took careful aim and fired shots into the belfries of the two churches at the end of the main street. Hearing the bells ping from the impact of the bullets, he gave the hoot of an owl at the top of his voice and disappeared into the bush — into thin air — and away from the law.

During the winter of 1914-15 Marie Girard gave birth to a son, but within a few weeks of the birth, she became ill with consumption and died. The child was taken into the care of a Mrs Alec Langevin, a resident of Biscotasing, and brought up with her own children.

The Army and an English Wife

Archie kept running. At the end of the winter of 1915 he was in Digby, Nova Scotia, which is over a thousand miles from Biscotasing and his brush with the law. Why he moved so far away is not certain. He needed only to have travelled 100 miles over the Quebec border to have avoided jurisdiction.

However, it is believed he spent the winter with the Micmac Indians and in the spring he had decided to join the army and had travelled to the nearest recruiting post which was at Digby.

Joining the army seems a strange thing for Archie to have done. The discipline and routine would obviously not have suited his wayward spirit. A sense of duty to serve his country must have overcome him.

Soon his shoulder length hair was shorn and he was put into uniform and one month after joining he was shipped to England for basic training. Two months later he was transferred to the 13th Montreal Battalion and sent to the trenches in France, where he fought as a sniper.

In January 1916 he received a bullet wound in his wrist and was treated in a field hospital and sent back to duty one week later. On April 24 he was injured again, this time more seriously. He was wounded in the foot and was sent to England to the Canadian Convalescent Hospital at Bromley, where the fourth toe of his right foot had to be amputated. It was during this time he renewed his acquaintance with his childhood sweetheart, Connie Holmes, who was at that time attending a drama school in London. For over a year he was treated in various military hospitals in England and eventually was moved to Hastings. He had fallen deeply in love with Connie and they were married at Hollington Church in the Wood on the outskirts of Hastings. Archie must have known he was taking a big risk. He was bound by law in his marriage to Angele, whom he had not seen for four years.

The marriage to Connie was not a success. He felt the same confines he had experienced with his earlier relationships. He longed for total freedom. He was his father's son.

Connie, who had been so attracted to the heroic image of the wounded soldier, soon found him to be a moody, sinister character, and at times she was just plain frightened of him.

After further unsuccessful operations on his injured foot, he was sent back to Canada in September 1917, for therapy and discharge. His foot was now deformed and he was given a 20 per cent disability pension.

His wife did not accompany him and after his discharge in Toronto on November 30, 1917, divorce proceedings were instigated.

RENEWING OLD ACQUAINTANCES

The Army Pension Board insisted that Archie should stay in Toronto for further therapy after his discharge, and he stayed there for most of the winter of 1917.

During this time he was to meet Angele again and during the four days spent with her, another child was conceived — Robert Bernard Belaney (Benny) was born on July 11, 1918. Angele had not seen Archie for four years and her simple undying love for this totally unacceptable husband really does take some understanding. She knew she could not change him. She loved him deeply and just seemed to accept her lot. When he was to leave this time she would not see him for another eight years. He left her with money and new clothes and was away again.

His desire to return to Biscotasing was overwhelming. He had many happy memories of the place, but his thoughts of returning must have been tinged with trepidation as he recalled his brush with the law and the attitude of some of the inhabitants over his treatment of Marie Girard. But the longing to renew old acquaintances forced these thoughts to the back of his mind.

And so he returned, cap in hand, apologised for his previous misdeeds, and resumed his job as a trapper, despite the fact that his wounded foot was proving to be a hindrance and lessening his efficiency. However, he was still a relatively young man of 29 years, and he soon began to build up his strength again.

Between 1918 and 1925 he spent the summers either fire-ranging or guiding, and the winters trapping, and during this time he slipped back into his hell-raising ways. As he feared, the memory still lingered with many of the locals of his neglect of Marie and his child, and of his drunken escapades of six years earlier, and he was much disliked by many of the people in Biscotasing.

However, one Indian family, the Espaniols, befriended him, and he spent much time in their company, and was made to feel very much at home by them. He came to regard Alex Espaniol and his son Jimmy as his adopted father and brother. All conversations between them were held in Ojibway, at Archie's insistence, and the family added much to his knowledge of Indian lore.

He felt so much easier in the company of Indians and he further intensified his attempts to be more like them. He dyed his brown hair black, and he perfected his Indian stance. Archie spent much time with the Ojibway Indians, and in 1920 it is said that he asked them to call him Grey Owl — and nothing else, the name that in later years would echo round the world.

He had found the town of Biscotasing a much changed place after his return. It had increased in size and the wheels of technology had begun to roll over the place he first discovered in 1912. Everywhere there was industry, as the white man encroached more and more into the domain of the Indian. It depressed him to see the rape of his beloved wilderness.

On his trapping expeditions in winter he was greatly disturbed by what he saw. There were no laws to protect the wildlife from the get-rich-quick operators who were killing animals to the point of extinction for their furs, which were fetching extremely high prices after the war.

In July 1925 he returned to Temagami, to use this as a base for guiding and hence met up with Angele and his children. His daughter Agnes was now 14 years old, and she got on well with Archie. Her pride in him as a father would have moved most men to stay, but nothing could keep Archie in one place and in September he left again.

Angele was to see him only once more after the summer of 1925.

Grey Owl with Indians

ANAHAREO

During this summer, unbeknown to his wife, Archie had met an Iroquois Indian girl from the Ottawa Valley who was to have a dramatic effect on his life. He was 36 years old at the time he met her.

Her name was Gertrude Bernard. She was 19 years old, well educated and very beautiful, and Archie was smitten.

He told her he was half Indian and had always lived in the woods and that he was a trapper, who guided in the summer. She told him of her family and her widowed father who lived in Mattawa, and Archie was invited to her home. Archie enjoyed the visit and got on well with her father. He felt good about the whole situation.

After he left he began to bombard her with passionate love-letters nearly every day. She was everything he had ever wanted. Her Indian name was Anahareo, she was a descendant of Iroquois chiefs and was Archie's epitome of the perfect companion. His respect for her was great.

However, the skeletons from his past were playing on his mind. He was beginning at last to understand his weakness with women. He wanted her so much and he sensed she felt the same way about him, but realised he could be walking into another confined space. Anyhow, bigamy could not be conveniently forgotten. He was in a dilemma. He could not live with her and he could not live without her, and he stopped writing after a few weeks. She did not hear from him for five months.

During these five months he had decided to trek from Biscotasing to Forsyth, 100 miles north-east of Quebec. On his way he had detoured to visit Angele at Temagami and asked her to join him, in a determined effort to help him forget his new-found love — and possibly to ease his conscience. She told him she could not leave her children, and he undoubtedly did not want them with him, and so, possibly quite relieved, he continued his journey. This was the last time Angele ever saw him.

On reaching Forsyth, Archie disappeared into the woods with two trapper companions, where he built a log cabin. He named it Pony Hall (Pony was a nickname given to Anahareo by her father), and then sent a telegram to her begging her to come and stay with him. She obtained permission from her father to stay for a week, and four days later she joined him. The romance flourished, and he treated her in an entirely different way from the other women he had been associated with. She slept in the cabin at night while he slept in a tent just outside. They were happy together as they told each other stories from their pasts. Archie told her the truth about his marriage to

Angele, his war experiences, and about his marriage in England. He told her everything except the truth of his parentage.

Anahareo was a very strong willed lady. She knew she wanted this man and was determined to have him and share her life with him. At the end of the week she decided to stay for another week, and then until Easter, and the weeks soon turned into months — and still she stayed, all the time ignoring her father's pleas for her to return home.

Then a chance occurrence led to what Anahareo later described as their 'wedding' ceremony. Two Indians in the area had been accused of setting fire to a trapper's cabin in reprisal for him laying strychnine which had poisoned their huskies. Although the Indians had every right to be angry, they had no excuse for taking the law into their own hands, and they seemed certain to obtain very stiff jail sentences. Archie was asked by the Indians to speak up for them and this he did, with the result that they received comparatively light sentences of 30 days.

Chief Papati of the Lac Simon band, to which the Indians belonged, was so grateful for Archie's efforts he insisted on Anahareo and himself attending a feast to celebrate his golden wedding. The chief was a deeply religious man, who conducted the marriage and burial services for his Indian band, and during the celebrations, knowing how Archie and Anahareo felt towards each other, reached out and joined their hands while the rest of the Indians stood in prayer. It was this simple act which Anahareo took to be a marriage blessing.

For two years they lived at Forsyth in their log cabin, each having to adjust to the other's ways. Archie was totally absorbed with his trapping and talked of little else, while for Anahareo the adjustment to his kind of life was harder. He sometimes found her a distraction to his work, but when she put it to him that she would like to accompany him while he was trapping, he scorned the idea, telling her it was a serious business and he did not want the worry of having to look after her on such trips.

Anahareo, however, was not one to take no for an answer. She was a tough, independent lady and through sheer persistence she persuaded Archie to take her along when he was emptying his traps.

When she went out with him she saw and fully realised just what his work entailed. She detested the killing of animals, despite his assurances that this was the only way he knew of making a living during the winter months. She saw traps containing only the paw of an animal chewed off in panic by its terrified owner in order to escape, she saw squirrels and birds caught accidentally. These sights were accepted by Archie as part of the job, but to Anahareo they were abhorrent.

Archie could see the effect it was having on her and it was agreed that all talk of work would cease in the evenings when they were in the warmth of their cabin.

In the summer of 1927, after a poor winter's catch, they were very short of funds, and Archie took a job as a fire-ranger. Anahareo was not allowed to join him and set off on a prospecting trip to Rouyn. Prospecting was something she had always been fascinated with. It was her overriding passion, and her great dream was to strike it rich. It was decided they would meet again in the fall at Forsyth, get their winter supplies together, and head for their winter hunting grounds.

However, her prospecting trip was not a success, and she managed to persuade the chief ranger to bend the rules and let her join Archie. They camped out all summer, and they occupied their spare time tanning hides and making clothes.

At the end of this summer when the fire-ranging job was finished Archie decided they would spend the winter of 1927-28 in the Jumping Caribou country, where he hoped to find fresh, unspoilt territory. They set off northwards, travelling by canoe, until they reached the edge of Attik Lake. With the temperature dropping below freezing at night they built their winter cabin and Archie prepared his traps.

During the winter Archie was to discover that the days of the trapper were coming to an end. The writing was on the wall. Archie had seen the signs over the past three seasons. He had noticed that the wildlife was diminishing due to over-hunting, and the price of fur had been falling.

They had a very bad winter. In past years they had made between $1500 and $2000 for their catch, but this time they only raised $600, which was hardly enough to settle the account for provisions at the store. His army pension of $15 a month was going to be stretched to the limit.

Archie's mood became despairing. As he approached the age of 40 he could see the way of life he had become accustomed to, slipping swiftly away from him.

In the spring of 1928 he realised his trappers days were over.

McGinnis and McGinty

Anahareo had long since decided never to be involved with trapping ever again. During an earlier trip with Archie she had come across two beaver kittens, whose mother had been killed in one of his traps. She persuaded him to let her take them home to their cabin. She named them McGinnis and McGinty and these two young animals were to have an important bearing on both their lives. Anahareo grew a tremendous attachment to the little creatures and they seemed quite happy to let her become their foster-mother. At first Archie merely tolerated them, but eventually he too came to love them as much.

With the decline of his trapping activities, Archie turned his attention to writing about his experiences in the country he had made his home. His desire to put down his thoughts onto paper was great. He had much to tell.

Soon after they had taken the beaver kittens into their care, they were joined by an elderly Indian named Dave White Stone, who had been passing by their cabin. He had known Anahareo's father, and after much talk of the past, it was decided he would become Archie's trapping partner. Dave took on the daily task of checking the traps, and this enabled Archie to spend even more time writing.

Archie was eager to find an outlet for his work in English magazines and had resumed correspondence with his mother in England. She had written to him asking his advice as her son by her second marriage, Leonard Scott-Brown, was about to take employment with the Hudson Bay Company in Canada and she was drawing on Archie's experience to give her son tips on life in Canada. The strange coincidence was that Leonard was just joining the fur trade at the same time as Archie was leaving it. The half-brothers were 800 miles apart in Canada but it is thought they never met.

In the course of their correspondence Archie told his mother of his ambitions to write and eventually he sent to her his first writings, *The Falls of Silence,* an account of a trapper's life in Northern Ontario and how the trapping trade was fading away. It was written through the eyes of a white man and the article was published nearly a year later in *Country Life* on March 2, 1929. Through some misunderstanding the author's name was given as H Scott-Brown. This was rectified in the following issue when a letter from Mrs Scott-Brown was published stating that the article had in fact been written by her son, Archibald Stansfeld Belaney.

The editor of *Country Life* was much impressed with Archie's work and invited him to send further material. By now Archie was corresponding directly with the editor and was beginning to tell him more about himself. He began to create an image of himself. He told him how he was adopted by the Ojibway Indians, but in no way did he deny his English origins.

The summer of 1928 came and Archie was again employed as a fire-ranger. This time, however, unlike his previous job at Biscotasing, he was not on the move, and was able to return home at night to his cabin, where he entered headlong into his writing.

Both Anahareo and himself had become more and more fond of the two beaver kittens, and they had become like children to them. Between them they decided they would move away and find a part of the country where conditions would be ideal for beaver, which was now becoming a threatened species, and start a beaver colony. The idea excited them tremendously. The irony of the situation was that they would have to finance the venture from trapping.

And so they journeyed by train with the two kittens to a small town called Cabano. Dave White Stone did not accompany them as they did not have enough funds to cover three train fares, and it was agreed he would join up with them later.

Archie liked Cabano and decided to use it as his base. He wrote to the editor of *Country Life,* telling him he was going into the woods until Christmas and asked him to be patient for more writing.

They then loaded up their canoe and eventually arrived at Birch Lake in the second week of November. In 11 days they erected a cabin, which was to be their home for the next three years. They were to spend their first Christmas alone together in the woods. The idea was that he would trap to earn a living, and at the same time, would continue his writing. However, his worst fears were confirmed, as no fur-bearing animals were to be found, and it soon became obvious that their income would have to come entirely from his writing.

Dave White Stone had rejoined them after Christmas and, leaving the beavers in his care, they took a trip into Cabano where they picked up a cheque from *Country Life* for his first article. This was the first money Archie had ever earned from his writing.

Soon after this they all moved nearer to Cabano on the shores of Lake Touladi for the summer, and it was from here they had to say farewell to McGinnis and McGinty.

The time had come for the beavers to answer the call of the wild and leave the company of human beings.

FAME AND THE SAVING OF THE BEAVER

The departure of the beaver kittens brought much sadness to Archie and Anahareo with Archie particularly sensing the greater loss.

They had changed his life. His attitude had changed drastically from one of killing animals to one of protecting them, and he found it difficult to accept that they had gone forever.

Archie's financial state was dire, and they often discussed moving to Rouyn, hoping to make a gold strike. They were getting nowhere, Archie's writing was not flowing as it should, and at least at Rouyn there was a chance of striking it rich.

The one dream which stayed with them was the hope of establishing the beaver colony.

Sensing Archie's mood over the the loss of McGinty and McGinnis, Dave and Anahareo decided to try and find some replacements. Together they trekked over 25 miles to a place where Dave had heard beaver were to be found, and the next day brought back two kittens weighing only a few ounces each. The journey was too strenuous for one of the little creatures and it died soon after their arrival home. Archie named the survivor Jelly Roll, and it was this beaver which was eventually to become famous through his books and films.

At this point a person in Cabano, who knew of their financial state and knowing Archie's enthusiasm and knowledge of the subject of beavers, suggested that they should visit Métis-sur-Mer, a summer resort where many rich Canadians and Americans spent their time, and where they could pick up lecture fees by talking about beaver, and showing off Jelly Roll as proof that man and beaver could co-exist.

They agreed to do this and after a long journey, and initial apathy from the residents of Métis-sur-Mer, Archie gave his first lecture to an audience of 100 members of the Ladies Club at the Grand Metis Hotel. After a clumsy start, Archie was in his element. The words flowed from him as he related to his enthralled audience stories about the Indians, their ways, their legends, and tales of the woods and forests.

At the end a collection was taken and an unbelievable total of $700 was taken. It was the largest sum of money Archie had ever possessed. The whole experience had been a delight to him. He loved the attention he was receiving.

After this success they returned to Cabano, and Archie and Anahareo parted. She left with Dave, still clinging to her dream of striking it rich, on another gold prospecting trip. Archie had found a camp 10 miles from Cabano on Elephant Mountain and he settled in for the winter with Jelly Roll and intensified his writing activities. However, he was still finding difficulty putting the words to paper. He decided to go back to the happy surroundings of their former home at Birch Lake to try to obtain inspiration to write.

It worked. The happy memories came flooding back to him, and returning to his camp at Elephant Mountain Lake he made a serious attempt to finish a book. This he achieved, and on February 5, 1930, he wrote to *Country Life* stating he had completed the book, which he called *The Vanishing Frontier,* a series of short essays about his experiences in the Canadian north, and he dedicated it to an aunt, presumably his Aunt Ada. It was eventually published in England, with several changes, under the title of *Men of the Last Frontier,* in November 1931, one and a half years later.

Meanwhile, Anahareo's prospecting trip had proved to be a disastrous experience. She had ended up having to take work in a mining company to get money. With enough saved she returned to Archie in July 1930. They had been apart since the previous September.

Archie had now found another outlet for his work in the magazine *Forest and Outdoors* and he wrote 25 articles for this publication between 1930 and 1935.

He was totally wrapped up in his writing and was becoming very detached and introverted and his relationship with Anahareo was beginning to show signs of strain, and in the November she decided to go to Montreal to find a job. Archie, almost relieved, raised no objection and settled into a second winter of writing.

During the year of 1930 Archie had written to the Canadian Parks Department suggesting they make a film about beavers living with man in the wild. He told them he thought the film would have great scientific value. A film crew visited him for several days towards the end of the summer and a film was made entitled *The Beaver Family.* By this time Archie had found a second pet beaver to look after and had named it Rawhide.

In January 1931 The Canadian Forestry Assocation wrote inviting him to be guest speaker at their annual convention in Montreal. After giving the matter much thought Archie agreed to attend, and he sent word to Anahareo that he felt alone and needed her support.

Again the lecture was a huge success. Archie was a natural. The audience loved him and the headlines in the Montreal newspapers the following day screamed out 'Full-blooded Indian gives lecture on wildlife'.

Archie made no attempt to correct this falsehood. He let the press believe he was a pure Indian, saying that he did not want to spoil their story.

It was after this lecture that he fell ill with pneumonia and was in Montreal General Hospital for two weeks. He eventually returned to Cabano on February 2.

Later that year a freelance writer named Lloyd Roberts, who had read Archie's work and was much impressed, was invited to visit Archie and Anahareo and see for himself the way they lived and the work they were doing with the beavers. Mr Roberts was so delighted by what he had seen during his visit, he contacted the Minister of the Interior suggesting to him that Archie's beaver colony should be put in one of the country's national parks, where the beavers could be given even greater protection, and that Archie himself should be made a Government officer with the post of naturalist or park warden.

The Minister accepted the suggestion and in the late autumn it was declared that Riding Mountain National Park in Manitoba would be the venue of the new colony.

The camp was to be constructed during the winter months and be ready for the following spring when the beaver emerges from its winter home.

And so Archie and Anahareo left Cabano in April 1931 to head for Riding Mountain Park, 276 miles north of Winnipeg.

As they left they must have reflected how things had changed in the time they had been at Cabano. Two-and-a-half years earlier they had been totally without money, and would have gone without food but for the charity of the local people.

Now he was a fairly wealthy man due to his success as an author. His film about beavers was being shown widely and his fame was spreading.

Riding Mountain Park, however, was not to be a success. The level of the lake was too low, and too stagnant to sustain a happy beaver colony, and so they set out to find a better place.

Archie found it 450 miles to the northwest at Prince Albert National Park in neighbouring Saskatchewan on Lake Ajawaan. He knew the minute he saw the place it was all he had ever dreamed of. He returned excitedly to Anahareo at Riding Mountain Park, enthusing over the new site, and in mid October they moved to their new home at Beaver Lodge, Lake Ajawaan.

The Times newspaper in England wrote an article on him describing him as a backwoodsman of Indian birth, and his publishers at *Country Life* were pressing him for more material they could use as publicity. In his correspondence now he began to sell himself, and asked to be referred to as an Indian writer. He gave his father's name as MacNeil and said he had been an Indian scout in the 1870s and had been a friend of Colonel Bill Cody (Buffalo Bill). He said his mother was an Apache woman named Katherine Cochise, and gave his own birthplace as Hermosillo in Mexico.

The transformation was complete, Archie Belaney was no more. He was an Indian named Grey Owl. He now signed his name thus and his bank account was drawn up in this name. He detested the name Grey Owl being quoted between inverted commas, and from this point on I will refer to him as Grey Owl.

During the winter of 1931/32, at Ajawaan, he started another book, *Tales of an Empty Cabin* and in February 1932 it was discovered Anahareo was pregnant and on August 23 a daughter was born — Shirley Dawn.

Grey Owl enjoyed his role as proud father and the new baby occupied their time and thoughts as the winter of 1932-3 passed by.

Towards the end of the summer of 1933 Anahareo took the baby to Prince Albert with the intention of spending the following winter there with the Winters family, who she had stayed with prior to the birth of Shirley Dawn.

This family were good friends of both Anahareo and Grey Owl, and Shirley Dawn was to spend much time in their care during her younger days.

The tensions in the relationship between Grey Owl and Anahareo had increased despite the arrival of the child, and when the spring of 1934 came, she found she could not bring herself to return to him, and leaving the baby with the Winters and not telling Grey Owl of her intentions, she set off on her own for 18 months to have just one more fling in the great outdoors. She could no longer stand the monotony of each day at Beaver Lodge as he wrote and wrote and wrote.

During the winter of 1933-4 he abandoned *Tales of an Empty Cabin* to write what was probably his best work *'Pilgrims of the Wild'* which told the story of Anahareo and himself and their life together. It was finished by Christmas, 1933 and he then went straight on to another book which he called *The Adventures of Chilawee and Chickamee,* a children's story based on his own experiences with beavers. This was published in 1935 under the title *The Adventures of Sajo and her Beaver People.* The book was highly acclaimed and the *Daily Mail* in England called it the best tale of its kind since Black Beauty.

Anahareo — Grey Owl's partner for 11 years

LECTURES IN BRITAIN AND AMERICA

Grey Owl's books were overwhelmingly popular. During the depression of the 1930s they were just what people needed. They stirred the imagination and gave hope.

He was in great demand for lectures, and everyone wanted to see the man in person. His fame in Canada was phenomenal.

In 1935 his publisher in Britain, Lovat Dickson, arranged for Grey Owl to do a tour of lectures in the British Isles. He was given maximum publicity in the British press, and lectures were booked to take place over two weeks at a small theatre in Regent Street, London. Grey Owl was to appear twice daily and although his first few lectures were delivered to a half-filled theatre, the word soon spread of this tall, majestic Indian telling his wonderful stories, and by the end of the first week police were needed to control the queues of people from all walks of life who wanted to see him. His presence was magnetic as he strode onto the stage attired in the full regalia of an Indian chief.

The tour was so successful it was extended into January and February, 1936. Grey Owl played to enormous enthusiastic audiences and in four months he gave over 200 lectures to nearly 250,000 people. The papers described him as 'The Modern Hiawatha', and 'The St Francis of the Indians'.

All the time he was constantly troubled by the thought of being found out as a fraud.

It was during this tour that he appeared in Hastings at the White Rock Pavilion and afterwards met his two aunts who had been in the audience and had kept his secret.

He was becoming an extremely rich man, making around $30,000 a year from the sale of his books and his lectures. Further films on his work with beavers had been made and were enjoying overwhelming success around the world.

However, he was disinterested in the financial side of things. He could not comprehend such large sums. He just totally enjoyed the adulation he was receiving.

He returned to Canada in the spring of 1936. During the summer he planned to finish the book called *Tales of an Empty Cabin* and return to England in the autumn of 1937 for a further lecture tour to coincide with its publication. The book, which told stories of the people and animals he had encountered during his life, was published in October 1936.

After continuing stress, Grey Owl and Anahareo decided to separate permanently. The parting was amicable, they both decided enough was enough, and she left Beaver Lodge on November 15, 1936 and never saw him again.

Soon afterwards, in the early winter, he was married again, this time to a French-Canadian named Yvonne Perrier, and she adopted the Indian name of Silver Moon.

The second British tour in 1937 was an even greater success than the first. He was accompanied by his new wife. The highlight was a command performance at Buckingham Palace when the whole of the Royal Family were present including our present Queen, then the young Princess Elizabeth.

He gave 140 lectures between October and December. The pace was hectic and very tiring, and under the extreme pressure he turned more and more to drink — but still he pressed on.

After his British tour he undertook an exhausting three months tour of America. Again he was a huge success, but his health was failing. He told a reporter that he thought another month of this pressure would kill him. It proved a prophetic statement.

However it was his wife who broke down first. At the conclusion of his American tour she had to undergo an emergency operation. When he knew she was out of danger Grey Owl went back to Prince Albert and Beaver Lodge. Someone had been left to look after the place in his absence and when Grey Owl arrived he sent the man away.

However, the next day he phoned to say he felt unwell and was taken to Prince Albert Hospital. He seemed to be recovering when he suddenly developed a temperature and sank into a coma. At 8am on Wednesday, April 13, 1938 he died, without regaining consciousness. The only problem seemed to be a slight congestion of the lungs, certainly not serious enough to have killed him, but it would appear all his powers of resistance had gone.

He died from exhaustion.

He was buried, according to his wishes, at Ajawaan Lake. His grave is marked by a simple cross with the name A Belaney running horizontally and the name Grey Owl vertically.

Within hours of his death the stories began to break. The *Toronto Daily Star* carried a story stating that Grey Owl was not the half-breed Indian he had made himself out to be. He was branded a fraud and a hoaxer. The press turned from showering him with adulation to dragging his name through the mud. They hated the thought that they had been conned. Every piece of dirt they could throw was hurled at his name. His unorthodox marriages, his brushes with the law, his love of alcohol, were all splashed across the pages of the popular press in banner headlines.

The dream was ended. The story closed.

Grey Owl, portrait by Karsh (Copyright by Karsh of Ottawa)

Summary

The accusations of hoaxer and fake have stayed with the name of Grey Owl since 1938. The disclosure of his true identity shook momentarily the faith of his world-wide audience in him and his work, and some libraries and booksellers withdrew his books from their shelves. But the interest in him survived through the war, and his books were republished as soon as paper again became available.

Unfortunately the uproar over his identity has grossly overshadowed his considerable achievements. He may not have been the full-blooded Indian he professed to be, but one cannot escape the fact that his books were written from experience, and, if the deception was intentional it was certainly not instigated for monetary gain. He once said he would do anything to make people listen to him.

Indian or not, the well being of his adopted homeland, Canada, was foremost in his mind. He was genuinely disturbed at the rape of the country and despised the greed of the men who were responsible for it. Many times he warned that Canada was allowing itself to be destroyed.

His preservation work concerning the beaver, the national emblem of Canada, is much to be admired.

True there were sides to him which were unsavoury. His treatment of the women in his life could not have won him many friends. It is probably true to say that the lack of normal family life during his boyhood contributed much to his subsequent behaviour. Anahareo was the only woman who came closest to taming his wanderlust spirit. She would not allow herself to be treated badly by him and he respected her for it. Even she never doubted he had Indian blood in his veins.

He was not perfect, but then who is? His sin would appear to be that he wanted so much to be an Indian that perhaps in the end he really believed the lie himself. Perhaps the identity was thrust upon him.

The truth is he brought a great deal of pleasure to a lot of people at a time when they needed it most — in the depressing 1930s. He wrote fluently and instructively about the things they cared about and when he walked onto a stage audiences were uplifted by the magic of his presence.

The town of Hastings is now proud to be associated with the name of Grey Owl and in 1975 the gift of a plaque honouring his memory was received from the Ontario Heritage Foundation. It was unveiled at the Country Park at Fairlight where young Archie often played as a child.

There is also a commemorative plaque attached to his former home at 36 St Mary's Terrace, Hastings.

The good things Archibald Stansfeld Belaney did in his short life greatly outweighed the bad and that, surely, is all that is important.